NINE SERIES

All About Our Fathers

Vasiliki Albedo
Mary Mulholland
Simon Maddrell

Published by Nine Pens Press
2023
www.ninepens.co.uk

All rights reserved: no part of this book may be reproduced without the publisher's permission.
The right of the authors to be identified as the authors of this work has been asserted by them in accordance with the Copyright, Designs and Patents act 1988
ISBN: 978-1-7391517-1-3
NS 05

All About Our Fathers

Vasiliki Albedo
7   Sunday Afternoon
8   Halcyon
10 Carnivore
12 Liar's Paradox
14 My Father's Nose
16 All Things Must Last
17 Fear Response
18 Landowner
19 Dream Father

Mary Mulholland
23 Mantel clock
24 Feast
25 Army father
26 My father paints cities and landscapes
27 What we do when an uncle dies
28 Our silent years
30 My father's keys
32 Airborne
33 Letting go

Simon Maddrell
37 Gripped
38 the numbers on the kitchen wall
39 Whimberry Pie
40 Centre-forward
41 Lamping wild rabbits
42 The first rule of bird-spotting
43 Tree Rats
44 *God didn't create anything*
48 dad's dick

Vasiliki Albedo

Vasiliki Albedo is the winner of Poetry International's summer 2021 chapbook competition, and joint winner of Live Canon's pamphlet competition 2020. Her poems have appeared or are forthcoming in *AGNI, Beloit Poetry Journal, Magma, Mslexia, Poetry London, Poetry Review, Poetry Salzburg, Poetry Wales, The North, The Rialto, Wasafiri* and elsewhere. She was commended in the National Poetry Competition and the Hippocrates Prize, and has been shortlisted for the Aesthetica Creative Writing Award, The Bridport Prize, The Fish Prize and The Sylvia Plath Prize.

Sunday Afternoon

My brother crouches by a car with a grenade.
I am sitting behind him on the couch, my head
on my father's chest rocking with his raspy breath
as he polishes his gun. Our mother's in the kitchen
slicing onion into the tomatoes, oblivious to the M67
under my brother's thumb, as he presses
on the X button killing a couple of guys.
I am letting him take extra turns, happy

on this homely afternoon, with rain percussing
the roof and gunfire interrupting like laughter
in a sitcom. I hardly notice the disturbance
until the air cracks open, and I turn to see
the pane smashing, my father questioning
his hand. *I thought it wasn't loaded* he says,
as we search the balcony for the bullet
that almost took my brother away.

Halcyon

When I give my father my poem
he translates it to Greek.

Each word teethes
in his mouth. He insists

on the unknown: *precipice*,
I explain: γκρεμός, an abrupt cliff,

rugged mountainside.
In the afternoon shadow I see him again

as I did as a girl in the dark
of his office: lofty, daunting,

a gargoyle poring over his law books.
He continues, points out he thinks

a verb is missing. When he stumbles
on 'halcyon' he stops and looks at me.

Smiling, he recites the myth of Alcyone,
describes how Aeolus reined in the gales

for a week every year to let
his kingfisher-daughter lay her eggs

by the placid sea. I nod
but insist on the nuance of the English

word I intended. *Calm*, he repeats
and starts again with the myth.

When he comes to the silence at the end
of the page, it's like tuning into the static

after a glance at a report card or an indifferent
Christmas gift. *Did you like it?* I ask.

I knew almost all the words, he says.
Later, there's a sough

in his voice I've never heard
when he calls to discuss metaphor.

Carnivore

My father has blown out all
eighty candles in one breath.
We sit around the table gripping
our spoons, the cake untouched,
glossy with spit and cherries.
There have been courses
of tartare and dripping red filet,
a small mercy of greens for me.

We have already dissected
whether not eating meat is making me ill,
whether animals think or feel.
On the wall family pictures
an evidence board, their frames
the colour of bloodshot eyes.
Female judges make bad decisions
because of their hormones,
he launches, *I never lost a case*
tried by a man. He grins, a cigar
tamponing his lips.

You are 'Paraponiariko', a little
complainer, he says, flicking
the record on to the eponymous song.
Tells me how as a twenty-six-year-old
man he borrowed money to treat
his father's lung cancer.
All the way to the UK they hummed

the great horned god is dead,
though the growth had spread,
and all the doctors could do
was give him blood.

But it was my mother
who made dad's veins thrum.
She sustained us through the war
and the land she bought guaranteed my loan,
my father says, his voice in ashes.

Liar's Paradox

Cretans always lie, Epimenides of Knossos

I see the plastic mouse and think of you,
my frown like the smile of the cartoon cow

on a packet of cat treats. A response
I trace back to stubbing my foot on the toy

while on the phone with you arguing
Ottoman history. Now, this is part of our history.

The stumble. The conquering. Enslavement
and war. The minor cut on my big toe, a knot

tied to you schooling me
on the accuracy of recorded history.

Things didn't happen exactly as written,
I pulled the trigger, and you started

on Hagia Sophia. How she was gutted,
her painted saints defaced as idolatry,

this for the sake of some monumental
truth, or for empire. I didn't want to hear it

again from you father, who cast
yourself angelic in each retelling

of my memories, or else
couldn't recall. *It's for your own good*

you said, but then laughed
you I know I'm a liar, which reminded me

of a joke about Cretans, or rather a paradox
in which something can only be true if it's false,

and false if it's true. The cat chews on the treats
next to the copy of a mouse and blinks.

My Father's Nose

People always said I was my father
with long hair, and I liked it because
I didn't want to look like my mother
who'd lock me in my room for hours.
Even when my nose lost all sense
of proportion and grew
thick, with loud pores just like
my father's, but on my smaller face.
Even when my first love called me a witch,
and even later when a friend
told me I had a good nose
for cocaine. I liked it
because it was ours and recalled
those evenings we sat poking the fire,
when I'd notice the silhouette
of his nose curve deeper as he smiled
and recounted the story
of him riding his horse with suit
and a tie on to impress the girls.
Or the one when he lost
his sole on the street and a young
woman picked it up and ran after him.
Or that one about his grandfather,
who had the biggest nose of us all,
and who won a silver medal in the war,
fighting for Greek independence
with our national hero, Kolokotronis.
Whose heavy, wooden shoes

my father still kept, and in honour
of whom the family name was changed
from something meaning bread, to a word
meaning fighter, and obliquely, promontory.

All Things Must Last

Always off-white, from Bobo the stuffed
dog I shlepped to the first day of school,
to my cats, Lula, Bouzouki. My pets, always

disappearing from my room, all cream
sheets and milkweed walls. I couldn't understand
where this thieving farm was, or how it could hold them.
My dad only said, *just for the summer.*

Months later, he called it a favour
when after fifth period we got in his Fiesta.
I tracked 7NE for forty-four minutes after the turn
off the freeway till we got to a clearing.

Straightaway I could tell his friend was no farmer,
though his house was wooden, land boxed
with a multitude of pens. He wore a blazer and glasses,
held a silver biro, didn't smile, didn't smell of curd or grass.

Down a long path, and I knew it was nothing
but a filthy charade, when he showed me Bouzouki—
only a stand-in. Dad's fake friend
sat me on his couch, asked me ten, silly questions:

could I hear them, how often I saw them,
how bright they were, in Lumens, in Kelvins,
did they burn through that patch of missing
wallpaper behind my closet, did they leave him a message?

Fear Response

My father never put me on his shoulders, he put me in his car
speeding towards a rocky beach or a field of honey locusts.

With my hands in cold water, I speak to my inner critic,
wrap the exclamations of my arms around my back

until the parasympathetic fires. I remind myself to smile,
breathe, anchor. Tell your inner shovel to quit, tell it I love you.

In prehistoric times we were chased by tigers is a cliché for a reason.
Don't let an ambush of bills and failures roar you to the
precipice.

Talk over yourself, take the hero's journey from the sofa to the
door,
delete his number from the list of things that can be used as
weapons.

Landowner

You say you don't remember
the time you harrowed
my cheek with your palm

until I fell to meet your shoe,
a tyne of rage
at my gut again.

My friend from school was there.
When you were done she hurried home.
I crammed coins and clothes and left.

Two streets down, you found me,
rolled up in your car with candy.
I couldn't leave. You are folded

forever within. Sending me flowers
with the right hand, while your left
is over my mouth.

Nights, when I have no defence
you jolt into my dreams to plough
your little plot in my heart.

Dream Father

He stops the car. Our tinny-blue Rover stark
against powder. Butchered pine stumps,
their needles scattered, entwined.
The sky flakes inch-fat crystals like stalactites.
He climbs out of his seat and pushes
my mother and me down a ravine.
We land in a floury sump, facing the wash-line
horizon where he appears as a blizzard.

Mary Mulholland

Mary Mulholland's poems have been published in a range of magazines such as *AMBIT, Arc, Dust, Fenland Poetry Journal, Lighthouse, London Grip, The Rialto, Under the Radar* and others. Twice-winner in the Poetry Society Members' Competition, she also won the Momaya Poetry Prize, was placed in Kent & Sussex, and Sentinel prizes, highly commended in The Rialto Nature and Place, and commended or shortlisted in other prizes including Aesthetica, AMBIT, Artlyst, Aryamati, Bridport, Trim, Wasafiri and Winchester, together with several longlists. Her debut pamphlet, *What the sheep taught me*, was shortlisted in the Live Canon competition and published in 2022.

Mantel clock

Even upstairs I hear the ticking –
Sunday, the day to be wound, eight
turns keeps the pendulum swinging.

It's French 19th century, pretty face,
grey-marble case with a crack
the horologist caused, yet it makes
me feel I let them down,
can almost hear their chastising –
father, grandfather, and the greats.

Though I baulk at most traditions,
winding is now a Sunday rite,
to maintain family ways
down the generations,
unspoken, written in stone.

Feast

He smells of gunshot, a brace of partridge in one hand as he enters the kitchen, papers the floor, and starts plucking, a faint pop as each feather leaves the skin, until one resists. He pauses, eases it gently without tearing flesh, and fills my shoebox with down from neck and flank, hackles from wing and back. Some he sets aside to make into flies. Taking a chestnut tail-feather he strokes my cheek, but I can't stop staring at the plucked-purple bodies, floppy necks, dead eyes in russet heads. He lights a match to burn the remaining fluff, chops off their heads, claws, and draws them, examines their last feast. I wrinkle my nose at the smell. *Barley*, he says, and lays them trussed on a dish. So small, so bruised.

Army father

I never asked if you killed anyone, would you have
told me? I'd peep round the door to your room,
you kneeling by your bed, head hung,
how your jaw clenched and unclenched.
I barely knew you, was afraid of your moustache.

When we were reunited with you after months apart
you had a dog, said it was part-Labrador, part-wolf.
None of us liked it. Not sure you did either.
I overheard you'd saved it.
                         I didn't think much
about the war, life or death, but would
smell the rotten waft of its tinned meat,
swiftly devoured, drool dripping down canines. You
said it was only doing its dog thing.

You'd take dog and me to Kyrenia, point out vulture,
viper, scorpion, the solace of being away
from the fighting, the quiet of your breath broken by
whistling nostrils.
                    Now I'm tidying the garden
for your funeral and a woodpigeon lands beside me.

In my head you're saying it's defending its territory,
calling for mate and family: *my heart bleeds b–ty,*
my heart bleeds b–ty, my heart bleeds b–ty, my

My father paints cities and landscapes

For over an hour he stares across sun-bleached
terraces to Mtafa, his smoke-blue eyes blinking
beneath a fixed frown, studying how light falls
on distant sandstone. Then the tinkling as his brush
clouds the glass, and he draws the sable over
raw, a glistening line. A dip of water before
adding burnt and cobalt blue to make a brown
mess of the white enamel lid, in contrast
to the mathematical clarity of his buildings.
As if he's intent on settling the conflict between
shadow and light, giving each its space. Spare brushes
like soldiers in a row. I ask why he never paints
people, and he makes me stand by the oleander,
for an age, my hand raised towards a bird
that's not there.

What we do when an uncle dies

We bring cake for my mother's sister, recently widowed,
stand in the doorway: my father, my mother and me.
I hold the chocolate cake I helped make, remembering
my uncle, the spy, who gave me coins from Arabia.
My aunt is dancing, all alone,
The Beatles on her gramophone,
she beckons my parents to join her, and
my father, so correct, starts jiving and laughing.
He reaches to my mother, but she pulls away.
Come on, he says, *let your hair down. It's the twist.*
She shakes her head, and the record sticks:
Come on Come on Come on Come on

Our silent years

i
Where did you go as you sat one side
of the fire, my mother on the other,
Tchaikovsky filling the air with a symphony
renamed pity? Your fingertips sounded a beat
as you gazed at something I couldn't see.
Once I told my sister I was the cause,
and you came to tuck me up in bed.
I said *goodnight*. The first word I'd spoken
to you in a year. Later I threw off
the covers, cried myself to sleep,

remembering claps of gunfire,
fireworks, and inside the mosquito-netted
curtains, behind the music, the silence
of a different kind of war.
It's always about taking sides.

Now I see it was never my war with you.
When I was a child we lived in a divided country.

ii
And here's a black and white of you
as a boy, fishing rod and jam-jar
by your feet, in long socks, shorts,
tweed cap, hands behind your back,
chin raised, staring ahead with the boldness
of a five-year-old prepared to challenge
whatever the future held.

The future has no sound of its own,
only the past echoes.

iii
Now, by the riverbank I find white-legged
crayfish, rove beetles, pea mussels, whorl snails,
water boatmen, hind legs like oars,
crowfoot's green hair rooted on silver stones.

A dragonfly hovers blue over bubbles
brown trout lay eggs on sunken branches.
The peace you found with flies
you'd tie, damsel, mayfly, spider, gnat.

The swish as you cut the air with a cast,
the stillness of a straight line crossing water.

Today would have been too bright for fishing,
but you'd have liked the silence,
nature's silence: birdsong, insects.
Then from the eddy a brilliant splash –

a yellowish mouth with creamy chin
bursts out of the depths,
snaps with tiny teeth at a fly,
disappears.

My father's keys

It started with house-keys,
losing them
or using the wrong ones,
striding around with purpose,
until my mother patiently
found them in the fridge.

He overwound the grandfather clock,
broke the lock on the back door
took it apart then couldn't
put it together again,
started dismantling all
the clocks and locks
in his drive to remember
he was an engineer.

We hid the car keys
for he no longer understood
speed limits and zebra crossings.
We sold the car, and he'd go walking
till the police brought him back
from the next county.

He would stare at the newspaper
as if it was a code to decipher,
then turn to the piano,
the same three chords.
She'd sigh, watching

him fall apart,
until it killed her.

He waited for her to return.
Each time we told him he said he was glad
she'd not had to suffer.

Airborne

Tell me about when they dropped you and you flew
to the mud-banks of the Ijssel near Arnhem,
scarcely more than a child, with parachute wings.

By your bedside you still have a book: *The Psychology
of Fear: How to Overcome It*. First Edition, well-thumbed.
What was it like to be dropped and to fly?

I heard your landing was softened by bodies.
Operation Market Garden. What are your memories
of that child who flew with ivory parachute wings?

When I took you back, we watched geese gliding,
effortless, to the banks, rising again. Unlike when
they dropped you and your friends behind the lines.

And now, each night with helmet and truncheon
you prowl the house – they're invading upstairs,
coming after that child with ivory parachute wings.

We take tea outside, like when I was the child.
I hand you a dandelion, we watch the seeds fall –
they've dropped you, and you're flying –
scarcely more than a child, with parachute wings.

Letting go

I didn't want to give my father a bath.
He didn't want it either. *Why don't you
have a bath,* he said and pushed me
into the water, his hand behind my head.

I didn't want to change wet sheets,
heard the crash of him falling, but finished
bundling the covers. Found him in a heap
at the foot of the stairs. He seemed fine
but I called the paramedics. When he tried
to bite them, they grew more concerned
about me. I said I was fine.

I don't know why he used to frighten me.
These days he's a child I don't want to have
to look after.

I put him in a home to go on holiday.
On my return he has broken ribs, pneumonia.
I take him to hospital, read him poems
about letting go. His eyes stay shut, his brow
furrows. A nurse sits on his other side,
suggests I take him home, make a bedroom
on the ground floor. I speak across him, *I can't
understand why he's holding on –
as if he's forgotten to go.*
The nurse says, *you know he's listening.*
I knew he was listening.

Simon Maddrell

Simon Maddrell is a queer Manx man, thriving with HIV and living in Brighton & Hove. He's published in sixteen anthologies and numerous publications including *AMBIT, Butcher's Dog, Poetry Wales, Stand, The Moth, The Rialto, Under the Radar, Ink Sweat and Tears, The New European, Morning Star* and *Long Poem Magazine*. Simon was first-runner up in the Frogmore Poetry Prize 2020 and highly commended in The Winchester Poetry Prize 2021. In 2020, he was longlisted in The Rialto Nature and Place Competition. Simon's debut pamphlet, *Throatbone*, was published by UnCollected Press in July 2020. *Queerfella* jointly-won The Rialto Open Pamphlet Competition, 2020. Simon's upcoming 2023 pamphlets are *Isle of Sin* from Polari Press in March and *The Whole Island* published by Valley Press in July.

Gripped

Father's vice-like grip
on my chin, combing straight
my sad partings & licking
his index-finger to rub in
that smudge
where I was christened.

Father's vice-like grip
on my youth, hidden
in semen-stained sheets
after nights of Rorschach-
blot awakenings.

Okay then Smiler, stay still!

the numbers on the kitchen wall

multiple times tables recited
games no sibling could win

an order of beatings top to bottom
the father's knee clicks on the fourth step

from the foot she looks
up at the shadow she sent

upstairs like a hired hand
forgetting four china cups

break like loose milk teeth
a torch through the sheets

one yellow-stained nylon
six books lay spread open

two butt cheeks left
modesty coloured

as he went for his sister

Whimberry Pie

Scrambling, stooping on camouflaged moor
        military searching after Sunday rituals
no-one goes home until the brass bucket fills
        tasks of tiny whimberries last beyond
dusky shadows sprinkling our pink faces,
        evening air breezed over each bronzed arm,
hair tingling, a thought of what was to come.

Golden pie deluged in custard,
        my drenched smile tinged with crust.

When summer berries outgrew apple blossom
        worlds collided — wild brambles in my mind,
it was the autumn of our content
        despite those things that were not,
it was the season of crumbles
        fed by blushed Bramleys
and every black hedgerow we could find.

Crimson-stained hands eager to finish —
        Grandpa's blood knuckles in the smithy,
hammer & tongs where fountain pen once was.
        Dad — nimbly tapping his keyboard — blue
eyes glimmer in the green-screen light of the night.
        Palms hardened by gardens —
now no kids are left to pick them wild.

Centre-forward

I arrived home, aged nine, with a number
nine shirt without a number
and a sewing machine without a mum.

Dad, a mathematician, back from the haberdashery
with a needle, thread and formula
fixed the hardest-to-number shirt of them all.

From two-nil down, the number-nine
levelled the game with right foot and head.
Breaking Dad's 'no-feinting rule' in a last-minute ruse
I skipped past boys with twenty-five yards left.
Dad's favoured-foot bulged the top-corner net.

Turning towards him, with hands held high
Dad was still mid-air, glowing.
I decided he would never land.

Lamping wild rabbits

Chalking gravestones with Dad tracing family logic —
inscribed, fading ancestors, crumbling islands of stone.
Polaroids of people gone, re-faced for posterity,
white-powdered cheeks, dust marks death on my pants.
Both watching gravestones falling out of the colour TV,
tombs advertising AIDS cracking the mantelpiece,
Rock Hudson's *Dynasty* crashing the spotlight,
those disowned corpses engraved nowhere.
Nowhere to hide, like lamping wild rabbits,
headlight executions reflecting my fear
of *myxomatosis* spreading, swollen-eyed deaths
of epidemic proportions discussed in armchairs
with Dad, puffing his care for island burrows.
Ravaging wild rabbits, sea kale desolated
at Prospect Cottage, like Derek. *Sebastiane*
and *Caravaggio* my celluloid palliation in VHS.
HIV — a greater rabbit-shocked fate, but still
my gravestone stands, waiting, chiselled,
painted peacock pink.

The first rule of bird-spotting

was simple enough. Unless you were sure,
one hundred per cent, you couldn't lay claim
to a thing, never mind win a point.

After just seven days on safari, father
scored one hundred and nine, with me
behind on ninety-nine, perhaps because
I was late to what was really going on.

To be certain about anything, we rely
on colours, on spots, stripes or bands,
the hood-eared, bearded or crest & tail,
the shape of its beak, coverts & flanks

including *what-can-only-be-seen-in-flight*.
How it might not be the place you'd expect
to find it. This requires patience, quietness,
some might say love — but love would mean

that every thing is a bird with feathers,
even guilt about the great spotted woodpecker
on my Flower Power balls, how I didn't know
his gender or proper full name.

Tree Rats

Dad wouldn't even call longtails that,
smirching grey squirrels for ruining
birds' lives & killing their red namesakes.
From a hospital bed, he sent instructions
to save a gnome in overgrown
borders, thinking he'd never
return. Later, in his armchair,
he was painting him & making him
a rod & fish. Now, in his memory,
by the birdbath, stands Albert,
an unpainted twin, and cousin Walter
with his plastic russet hat, who
grey squirrels knock over every day,
and then, they stopped.

God didn't create anything

in this world without a cure
says my father.
A solution he prescribed
rubbing the dock leaves
on my naked stings, or perhaps
that is memory playing with hope
and he handed them to me instead
simply pointing out this fact
with his pulpit certainty.

Conversion Therapy
definitely a solution
my father would have handed to me
if I had told him, or perhaps
that is memory playing with fears
in this world without a cure.

God Therapy
definitely a solution
my father would have prescribed
if I had told him
before his cancer from computers.
The doctor said there was no cure,
that God didn't create anything.
It took him seventy years to say
there's no need for that anymore
with his pulpit certainty.

Talking Therapy
definitely not a solution
my father would have prescribed
with his pulpit certainty.
If I had told him
nor would he have prescribed
to listening therapy either.
My mother left him twenty years after
they fell in love in Manchester.
It took my father ten years to say
there's no need for that anymore.

Diversion Therapy
After my brother died
my father buried him twice
in this world without a cure
for losing your own child.
He got up at 3am to wring
his hands, to rock in his head.
It took my father ten years to talk
about losing his child
in this world without a cure.

Suicide Therapy
At the same time in Manchester
the truth fell and broke my life
in this world without a cure.
If I had told him
simply pointing out this fact
I often wonder what
my father would have prescribed
after he knew there was no cure
for losing your own child.

Aversion Therapy
the cause is also the treatment.
It took my father thirty years
rubbing his naked stings
as if I had told him, or perhaps
after he knew there was no cure.
It took my father thirty years to say
with his pulpit certainty, *I told the chaplain
it's only practising homosexual ministers.*

Radiation Therapy
My father never talked about Alan Turing
but he studied computing at the same time
as he fell in love in Manchester.
It took my father fifty years
of exposure to radiation
for his cancer from computers
or perhaps it is a coincidence that
the cause is also the treatment.
In this world without a cure
God didn't create anything.

Plant Therapy
At the same time in Manchester
the cancer fell and broke his arm
the doctor said there was no cure.
I rubbed his naked arm
with comfrey leaves I cooked,
definitely a binding solution
or perhaps it is a coincidence.
God didn't create anything
in this world without a cure.

Hormone Therapy
in this world without a cure
chemical castration befell the man
who fell in love and saved the war.
After he knew there was no cure
Turing took his own life
in Manchester at the same time
as my friend. Perhaps like Hitler,
the doctor knew there was no cure
for father's one testicle. He said,
There's no need for that anymore.

Chemotherapy
definitely not a solution
after he knew there was no cure
for his cancer from computers.
Simply talking about this fact,
there's no going back anymore.

Aromatherapy
the night before, the nurse said,
there's no going back anymore.
We rubbed his naked body
with frankincense oil, or perhaps
that is memory playing with hope
and we handled him with soap.
There's no need for that anymore.

dad's dick

battered sausage
covered in poop
i never thought it would come to this
i hadn't seen dad's dick
in forty-three years
and now it's twice a day

reminds me of when i lost all feeling
below the waist & shat my pants
they thought it was MS
gave me a lumbar puncture
like when they named dad's cancer
gave it an expiry date

what i'd do to wash his dick again
just the once

after Wayne Holloway-Smith

Acknowledgments

Vasiliki Albedo

'Liar's Paradox' appeared in *AMBIT,* Issue 232, 2018.
'Landowner' appeared in *Ink Sweat & Tears* on 26th June 2015.
'All Things Must Last' was shortlisted in The Brian Dempsey Memorial Prize 2017 and was published in the winners' anthology *Poems to Keep.*
'Halcyon' won second prize in the Oxford Brookes International Poetry Competition, EAL category, 2017.

Mary Mulholland

'Mantel clock' appears, as a previous version, in the *Bridges Anthology,* 2018.
'Airborne' appeared in *The Friday Poem,* 24th June, 2022.

Simon Maddrell

Queerfella (The Rialto, 2020) included previous versions of 'Gripped' and 'Tree Rats'.
Throatbone (UnCollected Press, 2020) included previous versions of 'Whimberry Pie' and 'Lamping wild rabbits'.

'Whimberry Pie' also appears, as a previous version, in *The Best New British & Irish Poets 2019-2021*, The Black Spring Press, June 2021.
'The first rule of bird-spotting' appeared in *Lighthouse Journal,* Issue 24, Spring 2022.
'dad's dick' appeared in *wildfire words*, Frosted Fire Press, Nov. 2022.

Also from Nine Pens Press
All About Our Mothers, Nine Series Anthology, Vasiliki Albedo, Mary Mulholland and Simon Maddrell, Jan. 2022.

www.ingramcontent.com/pod-product-compliance
Lightning Source LLC
Chambersburg PA
CBHW021133080526
44587CB00012B/1274